Architectural **Wonders**

Kansai International Airport

AIRPORT IN THE SEA

John C. Waugh

HIGH
interest
books

Children's Press®
A Division of Scholastic Inc.
New York / Toronto / London / Auckland / Sydney
Mexico City / New Delhi / Hong Kong
Danbury, Connecticut

Book Design: Michelle Innes and Erica Clendening
Contributing Editor: Matthew Pitt
Photo Credits: Cover, p. 32 © Haruyoshi Yamaguchi/Corbis Sygma;
pp. 4, 17, 18, 20–21, 22, 30 © Kyodo News; p. 6 Erica Clendening;
p. 8 © Bettmann/Corbis; pp. 11, 24, 26 37 © AP/Wide World Photos;
pp. 12, 34 © Michael S. Yamashita/Corbis; p. 14 © Owaki-Kulla/Corbis;
p. 29 © Derek Croucher/Corbis; p. 38 © B.S.P.I./Corbis; p. 40 © AFP/Corbis

Library of Congress Cataloging-in-Publication Data

Waugh, John C.
    Kansai International Airport : airport in the sea / John C. Waugh.
    p. cm.—(Architectural wonders)
    Summary: Discusses the history, purpose, and maintenance of Japan's
Kansai International Airport, including what it is like to land on a
man-made island.
    ISBN 0-516-24079-X (lib. bdg.)—ISBN 0-516-25909-1 (pbk.)
    1. Kansai Shin Kokusai Kåukåo—Juvenile literature. 2. Artificial
islands—Japan—Osaka Bay—Juvenile literature. [1. Kansai International
Airport. 2. Airports—Design and construction. 3. Artificial
islands—Japan. 4. Islands—Japan.] I. Title. II. Series.

    TL726.7.J32K559 2004
    629.136'0952'183—dc22

                                                        2003012048

1 2 3 4 5 6 7 8 9 10 R 13 12 11 10 09 08 07 06 05 04

Contents

Introduction

Japan was considered to be too crowded for a new airport. To solve this problem, a man-made island was built.

As your airplane descends toward the blue-green Pacific Ocean, you look out the window. An island comes into view. You can tell that this is no normal island, though. This island's shape is rectangular. It looks like a very long box. Strangest of all, it wasn't made by Mother Nature. It was made by human beings!

For a few nervous moments, it seems your airplane will land right on the water. At the last possible moment, though, its wheels touch down on the runway. You and the other passengers breathe a sigh of relief.

You've just landed at Japan's Kansai International Airport. This airport is the first to be located on an island entirely designed and built by people. Each year, twenty million air travelers rely on this floating airport.

Planning for Kansai Airport began around 1970. It took the hard work of engineers, architects, and business leaders. It was an intense, demanding job. It was also an expensive job. Billions of dollars were poured into building the airport. By 1994, Kansai Airport was finally open for business. It's an architectural marvel—in a place where there had been only ocean waves before.

chapter one

Nature's Dangers

China

Russia

Wakkanai

Sapporo

Hakodate

Aomori

North
Korea

Akita

**SEA OF
JAPAN**

JAPAN

South
Korea

Kanazawa

■TOKYO

Hiroshima **Kobe** **Kyoto** **Nagoya**

Kochi **Osaka**

Nagasaki

Kagoshima OSAKA BAY

Osaka Bay, which lies between
the cities of Osaka and Kobe,
was chosen as the best location
for Kansai Airport.

**PACIFIC
OCEAN**

Tough Problems

Japan is a tiny, crowded nation made up of many islands. The country has few natural resources. More than half of Japan is too mountainous to farm. Japan must import raw materials such as oil and steel to make money. Workers manufacture products from these raw materials. These products, which include things such as cars and electronics, are then sold to other countries.

Many regions in Japan depend on airports and shipping ports for their economy to succeed and grow. These ports bring in raw materials from other countries. Finished products sold to other countries are shipped out from the ports.

Kobe and Osaka, two of Japan's most populated cities, are located in the Kansai region. Both of these cities depend on the money they make from manufacturing products. Decades ago, planners began to see that this fast-growing region would soon need a large airport. This was the only way that the Kansai region would be able to handle the traffic of people and goods.

Recipe for Disaster

Building an airport in this region was easier said than done. Japan has the seventh highest population

Many Japanese were outraged by the government plan to build the airport in Narita. The riots that followed led to twenty deaths.

of any nation in the world. Yet its land area is smaller than the state of California. Because of this, land in Japan has a very high value. Those who already own land don't want to give it up.

In 1978, this lesson was learned the hard way. That year, a new airport was being constructed near

Japan's capital city of Tokyo. The airport was built in a farming village called Narita. To build this new airport, the Japanese government took land away from farmers. This was done against the farmers' will, and many of them felt cheated. Some grew so angry and bitter that they took part in violent riots. They did this to protest the unfair treatment. Protesters set fire to buildings. People died in the riots. The opening of Narita's airport was delayed for ten years. Over a billion dollars was wasted.

Leaders in Kobe and Osaka did not want to follow Narita's example. They decided not to force people off their land. This left only one solution—Kansai Airport would have to be built on the ocean. While this would protect farmland, it would disturb some fishing areas. Government leaders paid money to those fishermen who would lose some of their business.

On Shaky Ground

Japan's location makes it an easy target for different kinds of natural disasters. It lies on fault lines that run under the Pacific Ocean. Deadly earthquakes often jolt this unstable area. In 1923, the Great Kanto earthquake hit Japan. It claimed more than 140,000 lives.

Earthquakes aren't the region's only natural danger. Coastal Japan is in the path of powerful typhoons. These violent sea storms whip up dangerous winds. Typhoon winds are capable of wrecking buildings, flattening forests, and destroying bridges.

Planners faced yet another problem. They decided to build Kansai Airport in Osaka Bay. However, the floor of this bay is soft, muddy clay. People feared that a major earthquake might cause the clay to shift. Would this set off a chain reaction, damaging or destroying the artificial island?

The planners of Kansai Airport were also concerned that the island's tremendous weight might cause even more problems. The island's weight would put the soft clay under a huge amount of stress. It would probably compress the clay up to 25 feet (7.6 meters). This compression would cause the island to sink.

BUILDING BLOCKS

Japan can expect a major earthquake roughly every seventy years. Smaller tremors shake the nation many times a month.

Typhoons such as this one blend driving rains with high-speed gusts of wind.

Troubleshooting

Constructing Kansai Airport was going to present many challenges. Experts began studying ways to solve these challenges. Geologists studied the ocean floor.

11

Engineers decided what materials should go into making the island. The materials would have to be strong enough to resist waves, water, and earthquakes. Accountants calculated how much material would be

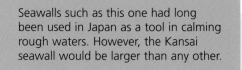

Seawalls such as this one had long been used in Japan as a tool in calming rough waters. However, the Kansai seawall would be larger than any other.

needed and what these materials would cost. Transportation experts studied how large the island should be to provide enough space for jumbo jets.

These experts began to develop a plan for making their dream a reality. A seawall would be built to hold back the waves. At the same time, material to make the island would be brought in. The island and the seafloor would need to be made stable. This stability would ensure that Kansai could fight the forces of nature. Finally, a specially designed runway along with specially designed buildings would have to be built.

Designers and engineers now knew what problems they faced. What they didn't know was whether they'd be able to handle all the problems.

chapter two

An Island
Is Born

When it was built in 1870, the Cape
Hatteras Lighthouse stood 1,500 feet
(460 m) from the Atlantic Ocean.
By 1987 it was only 160 feet (49 m)
from the water's edge. The lighthouse
is the tallest brick lighthouse in the
United States.

Wall Against the Waves

In January 1987, the long process of building the island began. Designers knew they would have to defend their construction site against crashing waves. Sea waves have an amazing power to erode, or wear away, whatever lies in their path. One example of this wave action happened at the Cape Hatteras Lighthouse, near Manteo, North Carolina. When this lighthouse was first built in 1870, it stood 1,500 feet (460 m) from the ocean. By 1999 the Cape Hatteras Lighthouse had to be moved because waves had eroded the beach almost right up to its base. The lighthouse was in danger of falling over.

Kansai engineers had to protect the airport from that kind of wave action. They knew that many coastlines used a system of breakwaters to stop harmful waves. Breakwaters are walls made of huge piles of boulders. These walls break up the damaging wave action.

The engineers decided to build their own breakwater. If it worked, it would hold the sea back. The designers knew that large boulders wouldn't be big enough to do the job. They used giant blocks of concrete instead. Each block weighed about 2,000 pounds (1,814 kilograms). Slowly, the workers built a huge ring of concrete blocks. This ring enclosed the entire construction area. Blocks were piled high enough to rise 40 feet (12.2 m) above the sea's surface.

It took divers many months to place enough blocks to make the seawall. They often worked in rough, choppy seas. Sometimes the job's hazards caught up with them. A huge block that had shifted underwater seriously injured one diver. He had to have his leg amputated, or cut off.

The seawall's success depended on more than brute strength. Strategy and technology also played key roles. Global positioning systems (GPS) were used in building the wall. This satellite technology made sure the concrete blocks were perfectly placed. To keep the blocks from shifting, a number of 200-ton (181 metric tons) concrete columns were set at the seawall's corners. Also, over forty thousand special blocks were used on the side of the seawall where most typhoons would hit. The edges and points on these blocks would help break up the most violent waves.

At a length of over 2.5 miles (4 kilometers), the breakwater at Kansai International Airport seems to stretch as far as the eye can see.

With so much rubble being carted to Kansai, workers relied on tools and machinery that often dwarfed them.

Fill It Up

Finally, in June 1988, the concrete container surrounding the future airport was completed. Counting all four sides, the wall's length was about 7 miles (11.3 km). The builders now had a hole in the sea. It was time to fill up this hole. The rectangular seawall was 4,000 feet (1,219 m) wide and 2.5 miles (4 km) long. The water was about 60 feet (18.3 m) deep. Filling this area to build the island took a huge amount of rubble. The amount of material used was nearly ninety times the amount used to build the Great Pyramid in Egypt!

How much rubble is this? Well, imagine that gigantic dump trucks were used to fill the Kansai Airport island. If one rubble-filled truck was taken to the site each minute of every day, it would take over twenty-seven years to fill the Kansai Airport hole!

Of course, the Kansai team used vehicles much bigger than dump trucks. Day and night, monster trucks were used to load the rubble onto huge barges. These barges then carried the rubble across the water. To get all the rubble they needed, the project engineers had to knock down three entire mountains!

The rubble was crushed and sorted by size into three groups. The sizes ranged from big rocks to gravel to sand. Mixing the rubble strengthened the island's fill. This special mix would help protect the island in the event of an earthquake.

Divers were responsible for putting giant stones in place under Osaka Bay. The conditions they worked under were often dangerous.

That Sinking Feeling

Engineers knew the seafloor at the site was made of soft clay. As they dumped more rocks onto this floor, the clay became compressed. The water would squeeze out of the mud. In turn, the seafloor would sink. *Some* sinking was expected. However, the engineers feared that the island would continue sinking for fifty years or more. If this happened, the ground at the airport might become too unstable.

A parade of cars leaves Kansai
International Airport (background) after
its opening ceremonies. This photo was
taken from the city of Osaka.

Its buildings could crack and tilt, causing great danger for travelers.

Engineers wanted to get most of the sinking over with before the buildings were constructed. To do this, they sank hollow steel tubes into the mud. Then they used special barges to drive sand into the tubes. Finally, the steel tubes were pulled out, leaving the packed sand columns behind.

BUILDING BLOCKS

Kansai contractors wound up putting a million sand columns into the seafloor!

The sand columns helped speed the compression process. Water from the seafloor began flowing into the sand. This hardened the seafloor and made it more stable. The seafloor could now resist the rubble's massive weight and pressure.

chapter three

Building on
Sinking Ground

Even with the sand-stabilized seafloor, Kansai's planners couldn't rest. They knew the island wasn't completely secure. It was likely to sink more after the buildings were constructed. Engineers guessed the ground would sink about 17 feet (5.2 m) farther. The airport's construction would have to be able to handle this. Engineers and architects would need to design buildings that didn't crack or flood as the island sank.

Piano Plays the Right Notes

The airport's centerpiece building would be its main terminal. The project team wanted it to be both strong and beautiful. It had to make travelers feel relaxed. The building needed to be lively. Its design would need to lift the spirits of weary travelers. To design this masterpiece, they turned to Italian architect Renzo Piano. Piano has designed everything from bridges to cruise ships. His projects have won awards for their bold designs.

One of Piano's most famous buildings is an art museum. This museum, the Centre Georges Pompidou, is in Paris, France. The museum showcases Piano's creative streak. Piano's clients wanted

The Kansai team hired famed architect Renzo Piano to design the airport's standout main terminal. They knew of Piano's reputation for creating buildings that were practical, but also lovely to look at.

The terminal building at Kansai International Airport features high ceilings and lots of natural light. So much light pours into the atrium that gardens are able to grow inside the building.

as much free space inside the museum as possible. In response, Piano had the museum's escalators placed on the outside of the building!

Piano has a talent for finding creative answers to the toughest challenges. He didn't disappoint the Kansai team. He designed the roof of the main terminal as a series of arches. This makes it look like a wave or a wing. This is not only a beautiful design, but a useful one as well. It helps air move more smoothly from one end of the structure to the other. Air flows by following the curves in the roof. This removes the need for overhead machines, such as fans and air ducts. The terminal is quieter without these machines. Colorful mobiles constantly flutter near the roof. This reminds visitors that air is always flowing.

In the center of the main terminal lies a huge, four-story atrium. An atrium is a well-lit courtyard. This atrium greets travelers when they arrive at the airport. It is known as the canyon. Transparent materials were used to construct the canyon. Because of this, great amounts of natural light pour through the building during daylight hours. The bottom of the canyon features lush gardens and bamboo groves.

Built to Last

The terminal was also a marvel of engineering. It was built on nine hundred concrete support columns. Sensors were placed on each and every column. These sensors constantly report how much the terminal is sinking. If one part of the terminal sinks half an inch more than another part, a central computer system is alerted. The computer triggers a system of hydraulic jacks beneath the columns. The jacks lift those columns that have sunk too far. Steel plates are then slid under the columns to lock the change in. This minor adjustment keeps the airport level at all times.

Normal brick buildings couldn't withstand the small shifting caused by the jacks. That's why Piano had the terminal built using a strong, steel skeleton.

The terminal building needed to be very long and wide. Piano used an unusual shape to address these concerns. Piano's terminal building design allowed the atrium section to be very tall. The open space gives visitors and travelers an environment that feels open, airy, and free. However, as passengers move away from the center of the terminal, the height of the ceiling decreases.

Kansai Airport architect, Renzo Piano, also designed the Centre Georges Pompidou in Paris, France. About 150 million people visited the unusual-looking museum from the time it opened in 1977 until 1997.

Piano called Kansai "a precision instrument." He has described the finished product as "a child of mathematics and technology." It took six thousand

workers more than three years to complete the buildings and runway. Although it was a grind, the workers had to remain alert and focused. [That's one of
the reasons why they would exercise together each
morning before going to their separate jobs.]

Nature played a huge role in deciding how
Kansai Airport was built. The airport team
decided to use asphalt instead of concrete
in building the runway. They hoped this
material would keep the runway from
cracking in the event of a huge earthquake.

Other Special Features

Kansai's construction was full of other inventive surprises. These design choices helped make a stronger, more flexible airport.

For instance, concrete is used in constructing most airport runways. For Kansai, however, asphalt was used. While concrete is stronger, asphalt is more flexible. Asphalt will sometimes bend rather than break in an earthquake.

Glass panels that cover the sides of the terminal building are set in rubber. This helps them resist the dangerous power of nature's forces. About 82,000 steel panels line and protect the roof. Each panel is small enough to be carried by a single worker.

The bridge connecting Kansai with the mainland was also designed with safety in mind. It is built from steel sections called modules, weighing 4,000 tons (3,629 metric tons). Flexible joints that resist shifting, shaking, and wave action link these modules.

For Openers

By late summer 1994, the Kansai terminal was set to open. On August 29, the airport's opening ceremonies took place. It was a huge, star-studded event. Japan's

祝 関西国際空港初便就航
関西―長崎線 NH841 1994.9.4

Many of Japan's major leaders were on hand at Kansai's ribbon-cutting ceremony. Performers and puppeteers also took center stage to mark the moment in history.

Crown Prince Naruhito attended the party. Thousands of Japanese came to celebrate and show their pride in this architectural wonder. After many years, the vision was finally a reality.

On September 4, Kansai International Airport opened its gates and runway for business. The airport impressed the public. It featured a world-class hotel and plenty of shops and restaurants. Its terminal won major awards for design and innovation. Tourists came from miles around to get a glimpse of Kansai. Some flew to the airport just to see it!

The new airport was a hit. Soon, however, the forces of nature would be hitting the airport.

BUILDING BLOCKS

Most airports have to close at night. This is the only way that people who live nearby can sleep well. Because Kansai is 3 miles (4.8 km) away from the mainland, noise and air pollution from the airport never reach towns and cities. Kansai became the world's first 24-hour international airport.

chapter four

Growing Pains

A huge earthquake that struck in 1995 leveled buildings, power lines, and cars near Kobe. Kansai, though, managed to escape with little damage.

Passing Nature's Tests

In January 1995, the earth shook, testing Kansai's stability. A powerful earthquake hit nearby Kobe. Five thousand people were killed. Another twenty-five thousand were injured. The sea rose 20 feet (6 m).

The damage at Kansai, though, was minor. There were cracks in some sidewalks and in one pipeline. However, not a single window of the terminal was broken! Meanwhile, a few of Kobe's freeways collapsed. This caused cars to flip over and crash onto torn concrete and steel. The bridge to Kansai Airport bent a bit, but did not break. Renzo Piano's vision had passed a huge test against the rattling earth.

Three years later, in 1998, another disaster struck the area. A major typhoon hit the Osaka coast. Winds reached 130 miles per hour (209 km per hour). People died, streets flooded, and cars were swept away. Kansai Airport stood its ground. The airport escaped with minor damage. It closed for just a brief time, when the winds grew too violent for airplanes to land.

Dark Clouds and Sunshine

Kansai is proof of human creativity and willpower. Still, some dark clouds hang over the airport's future.

BUILDING BLOCKS

It is estimated that over a million people have helped work on the airport project in some way.

Planners had hoped the island would only sink about 17 feet (5.2 m) and then stop. Instead, the island has already sunk over 30 feet (9.1 m). Even worse, it is still sinking. If this sinking continues, the seawall will have to be built higher. This is the only way that damage from future typhoons can be prevented. The cost of such a move, however, would be enormous. The airport's price tag has already gone billions of dollars over what the planners had imagined.

Kansai currently handles about 130,000 flights a year with its single runway. Originally, the project planners felt that, by 2007, Kansai would handle 160,000 flights each year. A second island with a second runway was planned to handle more flights.

Construction has begun on this new runway. However, flights have not increased as quickly as hoped. The world economy has slowed down, along with air travel.

Destination of Choice

There was another reason for wanting a second run-way. Kansai's planners knew the airport would make more money if it became a hub. A hub airport is used by airlines as a kind of crossroads. Airplanes that have long flight routes often land at hubs. There, they drop off a few passengers, refuel, and take on

Some of Japan's top engineers have shown concern over how much the main terminal's basement has sunk since Kansai opened for business.

37

The more passengers fill the express trains at Kansai, the greater success the airport will achieve.

some new passengers. Then they take off again, headed to their next destination.

Each time an airline company's plane arrives or departs, the airport charges the company a fee. Hub airports have more takeoffs and landings than other airports. Because of this, they earn more money in fees.

To be considered for a hub, though, a second runway is needed. This way, flights can be rerouted in case of emergencies. Airports with just a single runway often face longer delays. For example, they can be disabled for hours by a plane with a shredded tire. If this happens, the entire runway has to be cleaned and inspected for debris.

There are even plans for a third runway. It would cut diagonally across the end of the first runway. This new addition would make an even greater number of flights possible.

However, there has been an argument about whether building new runways is a good idea. Building the second island and runway would cost another $14 billion. The money for both runways is from loans. Hundreds of millions of dollars in interest would have to be paid on these loans each year. Only with enough airline traffic can the loans be paid off. Some business leaders are worried that building a second runway won't be worth the cost.

Trying to Take Off

Some cost-saving and moneymaking ideas have been proposed for Kansai. The terminal for the second runway may not actually be on the second island.

At a conference in July 2001, the mayor of Osaka, Takafumi Isomura, presents his city's bid to host the 2008 Summer Olympics. If Osaka is chosen to be the Olympic site, the city's economy will be given a huge boost.

Instead, it may float between the two artificial islands. This would prevent the possibility of the second terminal sinking.

Some Japanese leaders are hoping to host the summer Olympic Games in Osaka in the near future. If this happens, airport traffic would rise, giving Kansai a financial boost. Still, it's possible that money woes might stop the growth of Kansai— something that not even a sinking seafloor and nature have been able to do.

Most people believe that brighter times for Kansai lie ahead. A second runway could add over $100 billion to the region's economy. This would be a huge boost to the airport.

Whatever the coming years hold, Kansai Airport's design will always stand as an engineering triumph. Humans have built other islands in recent years. However, they had Kansai to use as an example. Kansai's example has proven to engineers and architects that they can work with, and tame, nature's more violent side.

New Words

accountants (uh-**koun**-tuhnts) experts in money matters and keeping accounts

architects (**ar**-ki-tekts) people who design buildings and check that they are built properly

asphalt (**ass**-fawlt) a black, tarlike substance that is mixed with sand and gravel and then rolled flat to make roads

atrium (**ay**-tree-uhm) a patio or courtyard around which a building is built

breakwater (**brayk**-wah-tur) a wall built to protect a harbor or beach from the force of ocean waves

compression (kuhm-**preh**-shun) pressing or squeezing something

descends (di-**sendz**) goes down to a lower level

engineers (en-juh-**nihrz**) people trained to design and build bridges, roads, or other structures

erode (i-**rode**) to be gradually worn away by wind or water

New Words

fault (**fawlt**) a large crack in the earth's surface that can cause earthquakes

geologists (jee-**ol**-uh-jists) people who study the earth's layers of soil and rock

hydraulic (hye-**draw**-lik) when something, like a machine, works on power created by liquid being forced under pressure through pipes

innovation (in-uh-**vay**-shuhn) a new idea or invention

mobiles (**moh**-beelz) sculptures made of several items balanced at different heights and hanging from a central wire or thread

module (**moj**-ool) a section that can be linked to other parts to make something larger

rubble (**ruhb**-uhl) broken bricks and stones

tremors (**trem**-urz) a shaking or trembling movement

typhoon (tye-**foon**) a violent tropical storm

For Further Reading

Kalman, Bobbie. *Japan—The Land*. New York: Crabtree Publishing Company, 2000.

Malam, John. *Super Structures*. New York: Scholastic Library Publishing, 2000.

Malam, John. *Airport: Explore the Building Room by Room*. New York: McGraw-Hill Children's Publishing, 1999.

Resources

Video

Super Structures of the World: Kansai International Airport. Unapix Studio, 2000.

Web Sites

Airport Technology—Kansai International Airport
www.airport-technology.com/projects/kansai/
index.html#kansai3
Kansai International Airport is building a second runway. This site explains how engineers will expand the airport. It also provides an artist's drawing of what the expanded airport will look like.

Kansai International Airport—Official Site (English)
www.kansai-airport.or.jp/english/
Kansai's official Web site provides everything you need to know about this airport in the sea. It features beautiful photos of the airport, along with a list of all its shops and services.

Resources

Kids Web Japan

www.jinjapan.org/kidsweb/index.html
A site that provides all sorts of information about Japan. It includes fun facts and stories about Japan's culture, sports, schools, and history.

Index

Index

About the Author

John C. Waugh has published articles for young people in magazines such as *Cricket*. He is interested in architecture's mix of science and artistic vision. He has also written for astronomy and computer magazines. In addition to nonfiction, he has published a children's storybook, as well as science fiction stories and cartoons.